Wind in the Cave

poems by

James B. Nicola

Finishing Line Press
Georgetown, Kentucky

Wind in the Cave

Copyright © 2017 by James B. Nicola
ISBN 978-1-63534-364-9 First Edition
All rights reserved under International and Pan-American Copyright Conventions.
No part of this book may be reproduced in any manner whatsoever without written permission from the publisher, except in the case of brief quotations embodied in critical articles and reviews.

ACKNOWLEDGMENTS

Grateful acknowledgment is made to the editors of the following periodicals and web-sites where poems first appeared:

"Achilles" in *Binnacle*; "After" in *Verse Wisconsin*; "Allegory" in *Pennsylvania Review*; "The Anatomy Of Bliss" and "Space and Fire," in *Chaffey Review*; "Balloon" in *riverbabble*; "Band-aids®" in *The Recusant*; "Beast" in *Penguin Review*; "Birthday Suit" in *Red Booth Review*; "Book Jackets" in *Blue Unicorn*; "A Certain Disposition" in *Literary Hatchet*; "Churning" in *Roanoke Review*; "Cotton Candy Cancer" in *Tule Review*; "Defiance" and "Expectation" in *Wordland*; "Did I react too harshly?" in *Spindrift*; "Disposition" in *New Writer*; "Elegy" in *The Harrow*; "Engraving" and "Fade In/Fade Out," in *mgversion2>datura*; "Fiasco" in *Marathon Literary Review*; "Hel—," in *The Dark Ones* and "The Nether Waters" in *From the Roaring Deep*, both published by Bibliotheca Alexandrina; "House Guest" in *A Narrow Fellow*; "Hug" and "Stupid Questions," in *Willard & Maple*; "I didn't mind" in *Grey Sparrow Journal*; "I Saw You" in *Clackamas Literary Review*; "The Kingdom Between" in *Stray Branch*; "Lucy van Pelt" in *Caveat Lector*; "Lust" in *ShatterColors Literary Review*, revised since appearance; "Moth and Flame" in *Shot Glass*; "Old Folks' Home" in *Writers Haven*; "Shackles" in *Studio One*; "Spite 2," in *Miller's Pond*; "Stone Struck" in *Empty Sink Publishing*; "The Styx" in *Peregrine*; "These Tears" in *Plainsongs*; "This" in *Iconoclast*; "Torn" in *Westview*; "You see" in *2River View*; "Walt Whitman" in *Lucid Rhythms*; "War Years" in *Slant*; "Yet Another Day" in *Nebo*

Publisher: Leah Maines

Editor: Christen Kincaid

Cover Art: by Tuska - *Icarus 1970*

Author Photo: Lénore M. Rhéaume

Cover Design: Elizabeth Maines McCleavy

Printed in the USA on acid-free paper.
Order online: www.finishinglinepress.com
        also available on amazon.com

Author inquiries and mail orders:
Finishing Line Press
P. O. Box 1626
Georgetown, Kentucky 40324
U. S. A.

Table of Contents

Night Writer 1
Birthday Suit 2
A Certain Disposition 3
tear shed well dries 4
Burning 5
Elegy 8
The Black Cloud 9
Boxes 10
You see 11
Disposition 12
Stone Struck 13
Hug 14
The Nether Waters 15
By Numbers 16
Different 17
Semaphore 18
Pilot Light 19
Engraving 20
The Kingdom Between 21
Open Sesame 22
Wind or Worm 24
Heart and Darkness 26
This 27
One of Us 28
The river's frozen solid 29
Churning 30
Moth and Flame 31
The Styx 32
Silver Spoon 33
Cavern 36
Dagger 37
The End of Silence 39
Cotton Candy Cancer 40
After 41
The Anatomy of Bliss 43
Expectation 45
Allegory 47
Achilles 48
Cheyenne 49
Water Lilies 2 50
Balloon 51
Shackles 52
Lucy van Pelt 53

The Mind of the Beholder	54
Lust	56
House Guest	57
Basis in Fact	58
Book Sale	59
I Saw You	60
Fade In/Fade Out	61
Walt Whitman	62
A Single Rose	63
Did I react too harshly?	64
After I Wrote	65
War Years	66
Space and Fire	68
Beast	69
Strange Day	70
These Tears	71
Mean Drunk	72
Old Folks' Home	74
I didn't mind	75
Stupid Questions	76
Cutting Board	77
Band-Aids®	79
Torn	80
Spite 2	82
Again	83
Yet Another Day	84
Race	85
A Difficult Parting	86
veil	87
Weight	88
Fiasco	89
Book Jackets	91
The Quickest Way	92
Dance et Cetera	93
Defiance	94
Hel—	95
Dreams should fly	96
Retort to an Outgoing Love	97
At Last	98
Furnace	100
Fireflies	101
After Rain	102
My Heart has Been	103
Fast and Furious	104
Weston	105

My desire's a wind trapped in a cave.

—Theodore Roethke

Night Writer

This missive is the same shape, though not size,
as Roxanne's window, but you never saw
me look up and imagine how your eyes
might look on me, if I could only draw
them downward, downward in the gloom, or leave
a letter for your morning tray. There is
a distinguishing feature to every love,
I warrant, and a difference between this
dirt and the darkness: So this is not quite
pornography, nor poetry, only the head
and hand tumescent, spilling in the night
the blood as ink; only my face turns red.
I'll think of you holding this, when I go to bed.
Till then, it's time to die again, and write.

Birthday Suit

What I am wearing now
I shall wear at close of curtain.
My birthday suit's
the foundation
layer of a shroud.
Of course they'll add a tie, a smile, a coffin
or a kiln.
Meanwhile I've added bagatelles
to keep warm and alive
absent you.

A Certain Disposition

I cried red tears. Tear after tear.
On tasting them, then seeing
they were, in fact, though bloodless, red,
I laughed so hard I cried,
thank God.
From sadness?
No,
for Being—
glad
I had,
in fact, not died—
which turned them blue
awhile.

At last
they're clear,
the strangeness passed,
and still
I'm far from dead.

Nor do I feel these phases odd,
or the symptom of a madness,
but comforting as solitude:
feel, rather, in the mood
to smile
to know
the dark will
disappear
and full of senseless gratitude
to the likes of you,
and God.

tear shed well dries

tear shed well dries, cakes;
blood within flows uncongealed,
drains, restores. sighs

Burning

The unrequited lover
stands as he withstands,
without,

like a freeze-dried tree,
tall as it can,
struck in a storm,

blazing although rooted to one spot:
The strength of his roots,
the source of his tragic inertia:

Useful as a candle, glued to its plate, night and day,
or a sun, caught in the orbit-meshed daytime sky,
or a star, cool, distant, trapped in near stillness of night.

Pine being soft,
Oak hard,
he may be neither, or both.

The leafier his tree,
the deeper the day-cast shade,
and the windier the shimmer;

The woodsier,
the hotter the light,
and the smokier the ashes.

Yet any tree trunk's heartless,
as the core of a sun or star,
or the wax of the noble candle—

of value
only when used:
born to be gone.

But sometimes a wood-be lover stands beyond
the burning, and rises to shiver and lean again
and dreams of clever ways to burn. And sometimes

a dream's incised
as an epic
or well-turned trope

on bark, or pulp,
churned, pressed,
softened, hardened,

whitened, blackened
with experience, loss,
hope, heart, mind.

He, longer than the moment's match, the incident's candle,
the accident's tree caught in a swirl of misfortune,
than even the longest stretch of the direst war,

goes on, burning, yearning for that heart:
If barely noticed,
like a blended star;

if come upon,
as at dawn,
like a welcome sun;

if touched,
like a tumescent ember
in its ashpile;

if breathed upon,
like a spark, a flame,
a life.

A book's
the cauldron's issue
vapored from a soul

who loved
and desired, from the peculiar vanity
of having to be heard,

held,
warmed
and cooled

by—let's just say
I'm happy
you are here.

Of course
I've gotten ahead of myself.
For now

we stand
as noble as we can
and aim to rise

to whatever airs
supply these brief
wicks' cellulose breaths,

surrounded by fickle flashes,
occasionally smitten,
sighing through O-such-a storm

of electrical entertainments
smoldering anguishes
excruciating delights.

Elegy

Bring the darkness with you then;
Join us in complaint.
Do not waste those juicy wails
Moaning by yourself.

Spread the gloom and dim the light;
Entertain us all!
We will hear the tales of hurt
Life has meted you.

Heed no sign nor uniform
That says our garden's closed.
We are up for guests tonight
And have kept your room

Here, your name already carved!
Fertilize it well
With two loud lungs, one bloody heart;
Water it with tears;

Make us cry and laugh at once:
Slay us—please—again,
While you flesh the myrtled row,
Filling in the dead.

Don't be scared. We'll part the clouds.
Not now? Then, in a moon.
Misery loves company:
We expect you soon.

The Black Cloud

I shall not let it eat the light
and do the white one in
I've so much left to do tonight
and want the white to win

Boxes

Boxes of sounds train bearers not to listen;
of files crammed with snapshots, not to recall;
of moving images, not notice really,
    and not to chat until a station pause;

of children, not to moon outside their matrix;
of crows'-nests, not to cheer with bleacher fans;
of dial-tones, not to hop across the lane
    and meet the face connected to a voice;

of workers, not to parlay with a neighbor;
of prim-fenced houses, not to breathe new air;
of frozen meals, not visit grocers daily,
    but fold vestigial gardens into tar.

I often try to break these boxes—try,
in stanzas formed yet freeing. But then twice
a year, on birthdays and at Christmas, I
    am wrapped up myself, in a latest trend.

One day I will burst out of, or burst, all
these boxes, but must meanwhile box the dream
so wrapped and shiny, that I tuck it in
    the back of a dark closet and can live.

You see

You see,
that day was a beaded curtain
to a back room
where you could not go
not then
not then.

Though I had been
you hadn't
and I wasn't about to drag you
nor leave you there in the front room without me
not then.

All I could do was tell you
that that's where I'd like to go
with you with you
and let you think about it awhile
so that maybe you'll take my hand
or touch my robe
like Scrooge to Christmas Now

and we'll go
together
to the dark back room
one day
and fly
like The Present
and see clearer
all through the night.

Disposition

I think I was born with a tank of cheer
and would dose you with some
if only you'd dare to drink, my dear—
the fact you don't being my fault, I fear,
for insistently acting so cheerfully dumb.
But it's only because of the way you appear
from afar, about to change your mind, and come.

Stone Struck

It could have been the raven hair that made
him feel like Theseus: To rescue from
the maze along a winding, bright and gold-
en thread. How hot that day. How hot that night,

for he deposed the shiny shield of sense,
unlike Perseus, to sneak an un-
reflected peak back at the dark coiffure
of his beloved and saw there only beauty,
the snakes of guile invisible to him.

But he was struck, and since the rescue and
the meeting of their eyes, he has been stuck
in that position, quickened to the core,
unable to move. And he calls it Love.

Beware the beckoning beam of a seducer!
Where a citadel has been commissioned,
a snake nest on a monstress' head is almost
guaranteed to sit concealed behind
some panel, sure as the seeming gratitude
for the rash acts of a champion is so warmly
greeted, invariably misconstrued,
as luscious, warm, and unrestricted
interest.

Hug

A vulture's perched at his inscrutable
coign of vantage, within or nearby,
invisible, waiting to dart
and grab a meal from those I love
when my brother drinks or my nephew speeds.

I've tried to squeeze the demons out
of them by hugging well, for half a hug
is nothing. A kiss is nothing either,
or something that surrounds a nothing,
but, like the passage of a birth
or its fraternal inverse twin,
death,
the journey's made. Meanwhile

I hold dear what my Nanny said,
"Hold your children close with open arms,"
and apply the riddle to adults too,
when I am worried and can do
nothing else. I'm not sure of the proper
pressure to squeeze the doppelgangers out
and thwart the buzzard, but nonetheless

I try, again and again.
If there is Nothing in an embrace
but hope, well, Hope flies in the face
of danger, being the opposite
of Fear, and *can't not*. And I've felt
the flutter and flap of the morbid bird

and glimpsed in *your* eyes the desert gaze
of the ghoul about to spring to life
and would bind his wings and seel his eyes.
Right now. So come here. Embrace me. Tight.
Even while the vulture's watching, waiting, drooling.

The Nether Waters

As still as nether waters seem;
as cool and soft, moonfire;
as innocent, a walking dream
and calm, the evening air;

as easy as it is to tame
the animal beguiled:
this transient indigo's the same
as when the waters boiled.

While stars send lucifers of lights
a soft breeze starts to rise;
the Altogether reignites
a memory of sighs.

I think that I smell jasmine—or
am I imagining?—;
I feel that I've set sail once more
to life, to everything,

to you, who made the coolness warm
then made the waters rage
until the echo of a storm
restored me to an age.

The Stygian depths are stilled, of course,
and sailing's safe till dawn.
But I'm amazed how clear nights force
me yet to wonder on

what wake of stirs and currents there
might be, less innocent
than they appear, to take me where
the wilder waters went.

By Numbers

The twos define the bonds between, their line
segments like chance involvements: what pairs might
be forged. Draw all such links and you define—
or rather, since no image can be right,
approximate—what we've called God. That is,
the god of status quo. For there are threes
and ones to pry and add, plus all of His
undraftable eventualities,

plus wilder elements than Helium
Atomic Number Two (inert, of course),
like Hydrogen and little Lithium,
and other ones and threes. Plus unseen force—
centrifugal, centripetal, as grave
as gravity which pulls, and inertia,
resisting what new courses we might crave
for His unknowable, unpredictable law.

My dreams were wild, but were a part of me,
the present's present, wanting a future.
Unfortunately they could not foresee
the twisting of a bond that was as sure
as God's, I thought, or that you would prefer
to act as One awhile and spin off free
and light as Hydrogen. Or might it be
that we were never who I thought we were?

Different

If the timing were different—
    our season in sync, or more so:
If the spacing were different—
    you living here, I living there:
Or if the situation were other than what it was—
    our stirring not in such an official cauldron,
    its leaden lid bolted down with proper clamps:
And if the words had been different—
    fewer, or freer:
Who knows?

But I shall still applaud from time to time
From over here, unheard—I'm clapping now—;
Try my best, and manage, not to inquire
How you are doing;
And when I can no longer contain myself,
Write that O improper letter to adjust
    time, space, and situation with words that
    make all the difference in reforming lives
    and seasons, words which I shall never send
But turn instead into a proper poem.

Semaphore

I said Goodbye to you that day—
remember, it was May?
From the top of a stairway
   you turned and waved

before being swallowed by a doorway.
Then I was unexpectedly back in September.
You caught my eye
   and waved—

Remember?—
as if to say
in that robust way you had,
that I had no cause to be concerned, or sad.
Then friends of yours—were they friends?—dragged you away.
My final day, we met at the punch.
You said a sentence,
I said a sentence
like two flapping fools—no, that's not true,
I was the only fool. Not you. Not you.
The party thinned
and as you left
   you waved,

Seeyalater.
My hand with a will of its own
   waved back.

Your face looked like my heart. . . .

These are the strokes of futile flags
redacted in blue, revised in red.
The sequence resting on yellowing white
is fading from its moment born in black.

Pilot Light

> *You have turned into my memory of you.*
> —Anna Akhmatova

I thought a week's proximity would dowse
the pilot light that you'd left on in me
as time has been transforming you into
a memory of you,
of innocence, beautiful potential,
but faint of light.

And now I see a softer, clearer light
no longer blinded sorely by my own
and feel the heat from here, time-zones away,
and know I have to be the glaringest fool in the world

to think a mere proximity could help
me dowse the dying, valiant, clinging flame
you had declined to kindle or to join.
I had denied that you'd ignited it!

And now that time transforms me too into
a memory, I ask one thing of you:
Forget—let it grow dim, then dark, and cold;
Or, if you shall remember, keep it light
that it might bathe and warm you in a peace
in later days and happy years to come.

Oh, keep it, keep it warm, keep it light!

Engraving

I heard a bird from beneath a bush
cawing my name. Then it grew still.
and the wind went woosh

and died with a similarly sudden hush.
And then I saw, on a mossy sill,
like a terraced ledge (beneath the bush

where I'd heard the bird), in the mulchy mush,
a stone, engraved, wedged into the hill,
where the wind went woosh,

level and inviting, like a cush-
ion. I sat, then lay down, as stragglers will,
and inferred a bird beneath the bush

but heard no bird but silence. A rush
of my blood made me feel too mad, too ill
to move, so I lay where the wind went woosh.

Though the moss was a mess and the ferns were lush,
my name appeared etched in the stone—until
I heard the bird from beneath the bush.
Then the wind went woosh.

The Kingdom Between

Between the stomach and the heart's the Mammal,
which gnaws, and makes me feel, or think I feel.
Lower, between the stomach and the groin,
concealed in weeds and skulking, the Reptile.
Higher than either of these stands the Human,
between the heart and head. Higher still,
to Which the Reptile's deaf, the Mammal too
embattled to be bothered by, the Bird
with intermittent flights of hope or fancy
like surfers searching for the perfect wave
dreams of an effortless and soaring peace
that the rest of me, vicariously, might know.

Open Sesame

Decision time. A crossroads, or a dream
where an invisible monster has chased
you up to the mouth of a cave? There a giant
boulder blocks your passage, and the creature
is about to devour you. Now, it could be that
you are inside the cave, and must get out,
or it could be the other way around.
But from your gut you know a few things. One,
that once you move the rock and cross the threshhold,
you may never again be standing where you are now,
may never again go where you've been, be who
you were all your life, till now. So to escape
means to move onward, yes, but to forsake
what was, what you were. Two, the rock is light,
so merely mouthing the words OPEN SESAME,
if not a flick of a pinky finger, would
be adequate to displace it. Three, the monster
chasing you is the one inside you, of
your own making. And four, that the Openness
is Everything. What do you do, what will
you do, what have you done? And now the mouth
of the cave is the door we're standing at. The knob
beckons. What do we do? We reach and stretch
our fingers till they tinker with the thing
in an absent-minded languor, call it literature,
but feel that we must bolt! Oh, *Haste makes waste,*
but *He who hesitates is lost.* To add a third
trope, caught *between a rock and a hard place,*
which is the way now? Through the door with you,
through it *to* you, or stay and welcome you,
if you are on the other side? And for
that matter, who the hell are you? No, hell
is Not You, that's the other thing I know,
only I hope that you suspect that hell
is Not Me, and whichever way we go

there'll be another door, another knob,
another cave, another mouth and boulder,
and another you and me, another time.

Wind or Worm

Love—is it
a wind in the cave, or
a worm in the soil?
You tell me.

As a wind in the cave
it blows but is trapped
and so leaves detritus
from unexplored walls,
dust, soot, muck, mire
and crumbly rock
dislodging and felling
a safely tucked nest
of insects which
when riled sting
relentlessly but
unbearably sweetly
with emphasis on
relentlessly.

As a worm it grows
by eating dirt
and survives unhurt
when cut in two
and poops out hope
no matter what
foul thing you do
contaging every
thing with dark
fertility.

Until
    the kiss
when a sudden urge
lets it emerge
from the hollow or depths
(hello?) to somewhere

more—or less—
ridiculous

Like this.

Heart and Darkness

Your darkness is not special. It's perspective.
You thought there was the possibility
of day, in there? But daylight never reaches
a heart. Your heart. That is a dark place and
mysterious because it is supposed
to be. The light is for your eyes. For it
to warm you, it must reach your skin, heat there
before it can spread to your rest, the mysterious
and inscrutable parts of whoever-the-hell you are.
Even the earth, and other planets, are
only half-basking in day at any time—
and only on their surfaces. Beneath,

it's dark. So you have never been alone.
Rather, you are the universe. Or like
it. So if you would feel a warmth, let us
touch. Then open your eyes. And it will be
as if the light were let inside—simile
is as far as we can get in this life
as far as ever attaining in your guts
the likes of a late-spring sunny afternoon,
or a rainbow, after a too-long spate
of rain. If you think it might help, we
can go to the children's park and paint our faces,
repudiate the darkness in the heart

together. The togetherness makes it art.

This

I'll have you know that I did not want this.

I did not want This. Yes, had I foreseen
the likelihood of This, This would have been
avoidable. It's simple now to see.
But Not This was a possibility
as well. Or so I thought. And I thought That
was what I wanted. But That doesn't matter, nor what I did want. However, how
I got This, which I didn't want, I can't
know without more of This, a thought so daunting as to paralyze. To understand
will only waste more time. I know this now.

The question, in the best analysis,
is not *Is This?* or *Isn't This?* but *And
so?*, isn't it? To put This aside, break
This, move on full of This, or This in tow—
All these I'll try, and yet shall never know
if any of these is the worst mistake. . . .
If That were possible. So, moving on,

I take a leap of faith, a leap away
from, turning to a place where I might land;
That, turn at least invisible; and This
be only what I face night with, and dawn,
until the middle of the night or day
I wake up with a start and find it—gone.

One of Us

> *Who are you in love with? me?*
> *Straight against the light I cross.*
> —Frank O'Hara, "Walking to Work"

If

OneOfUs

were in love
with the other

OneOfUs

and

OneOfUs

saw the other

OneOfUs

on the street

OneOfUs

should   probably
   cross the   street
       one of   these years
          and make the   TwoOfUs
                in - to

OneOfUs

— or

Naught.

The river's frozen solid

The river's frozen solid. But you know
the death is superficial. If you look,
a world that's dark and lush still stirs below.

And you and I are aqueous, although
I don't mistake you, as you once mistook
me, for a river frozen solid. (No,

for steel!) But all year, blood and hormones flow
(too fast, at times: down hills, as in a brook
with, granted, less that's dark and lush below

than rivers which are mightier but slow
enough to freeze). And that time you forsook
me, I froze on the surface too, you know.

But underneath? Oh, it was never so!
Besides, what river feels? And what bad luck
makes rivers, dark and lush, still stir below,

what loss, what love? None. Let the season go:
Your surface shall melt, and your winters' muck,
like rivers', frozen solid. And I know
a world dark, lush—*alive*—will stir below.

Churning

When you are invited
to stay awhile somewhere—
with friends on a great vacation
or a temporary out-of-town work situation—
and go,

and grow to love a certain person
you chance to meet and spend some time with there
—of whom you'll probably think every time you think about the place—
well, you won't be able to help yourself from a sense of loss and grieving
upon leaving.

When that love's unrequited
and you can't help but care
and yet would put an end to the upheaving,
the day you leave may even be relieving
and make you less inclined to put a curse on—
call it, for want of a better word—despair,
and on the first day you ever saw that certain person's face.
But the heart will start to spin, twirl as in muck, and feel like it's churning,
on returning. . . .

No process known on earth can ever make
sweet butter from sour milk. Ha! But a heal-
thy heart, in spite of ache,
can, through agitation
day to day and hour on hour,
convince the head it's well
and turn abject degradation
into the sweetest, sour
anticipation.

Moth and Flame

The random danger in the way it glows
in tongues of light, fingers of heat, or both,
makes any flame attractive to the moth.
     Or that he knows

how easy it is to avoid its sting:
Day creatures do it all the time. But I,
smitten and nocturnal, could only fly
     into the thing

that's no thing, can't be held, only contained.
Now, like the daisy which some youth, to settle
his aching, has plucked free of every petal,
     I'm wingless and

howl nightly warnings upward at the sky
unheard by other moth men winging by.

The Styx

Have you ever been invited and then gone
to a surprise party for the certain one
you loved to death, who's unavailable?

A choir of fallen angels *Oooh* you on
a river trip, the gondola to hell
past stalagmites and stalactites of flames
and intermittent half-familiar names
that freeze you as they burn. The gondolier
won't let you out, and yet you know you steer
yourself—that you are he! Next thing you hear,
that loved one's dead of plague. AIDS. I know
of hell and heaven, see. They're the same place

and no place, where I'm not and am and go
unmoved save by an empathy of stone
carved shallow in relief to make a face
half human: Mouthing only to atone
for what I never did, it tries to sing—
for want of feathers, hope, an angel wing—
and yet can only squawk, devoid of grace,
like any ravished, ravenous, naked crow
remembering that oratorio.

Silver Spoon

There was a "silver spoon" who craved
    To stir, and left his rack
To pass as a prince in a pauper's world
    Clad in thrift-store black.

A starving artist you'd run into
    At Soho openings.
Free wine. You went for coffee
    And in time for . . . other things.

He never let you pay or split
    The check, though you were sure
He, unemployed, was destitute,
    While you were merely poor.

You told your modern friends of this,
    Certain they would wince.
On meeting him, though, they could tell,
    And said he was a prince.

One night he takes you to his place
    Down by Avenue C.
The block is squalor but his loft—
    Sheer creativity.

How talented, this self-made man,
    Bohemian and sweet.
It seems as if he worships you—
    He does, until you meet

His parents up on Eighty-Sixth
    Where he was born and reared.
They tell you of his family Name
    Whereof the world has heard.

They're smooth. They're good. They'd *wanted him*
    To forge his own life's path.

But after all he's Someone Else—

    The rest is aftermath.

                    * * *

Years later in the South of France
    (A town you'd told him of
And where together you'd made plans
    To go, being in love

Back then; now you are there with friends
    For the cuisine and art)
You meet him on an evening stroll
    And you can hear your heart.

He'd married well, some famous wife
    Who's left him famously.
His kids are . . . *grown and gone. Say, would
    You have a drink with me?*

Coincidence? Not just that he
    Is here, but that he says
The very thing you've dreamt he might
    For most of your long days.

But in his eyes, there's not just sweetness
    But that cowardice—
You ask him how his folks are, first.
    Both doing fine. That's nice.

*I'm sure they'd love to see you.
    They're just back at the hotel.*
And suddenly you're busy.
    And you wish his parents well,

And him, and kiss his cheek, and go,

And try not to look back.

For silver spoons are not to stir,
   But leave on the spoon rack.

Cavern

What cavern? Why, the carapacial heart—
so hollow, though, that I can almost hear
the wind there echo, fade and rise again,
emerging as the breath of clumsy art:
this sussurus air suggests I may be near
an opening, about to glimpse an in-
ner space, an outer, or a mystery,
where flows the source of every giggle, grin,
frown, inspiration, and idiocy.

It isn't often that it will appear,
but in the cruelest month that rushing flow
is sense-able and makes me want to go
through, feel where I am not supposed to be,
so badly, that I bare this part of me:
the Everything you're not supposed to know,
an Everywhere I'm not prepared to see.
Not now, when the breeze sounds like a guffaw;
I mean in early spring, after the thaw.

Dagger

Though invisible it pressed, the blade
that's honed as hope, sharp as the gnaw
of danger, double-pointed with no
handle, one tip enthralling you,
the other, me. Nearness kept it
in place as it kept us apart, half-whores
to Safety, suffering the lightning and enlightening
of breaths intermingled, on the verge of touch—

of more.

To step inward an inch, two inches, three,
would have conjured the silver-hued steel into a knotty
cord, presto, like magic—and yet
that rope would have bound us tighter, unless
it dissolved into air, or smoke, or turned
into a bright red silk. Without magic, though,
it would have remained a dagger, and pierced,
and drawn heartsblood at either end, if not

at both.

Without each of us believing in the spell,
I saw that a bloody mess was in the works.
That possibility of darkness, when there's love,
acts as an empathetic, yet dutiful, Chaperone,
who intervenes with the lightness of a nod,
the application of a weightless finger
applied just above the heart, near the sternum, or so.
She stepped me back to let the dagger fall.
I still hear the embarrassing, clumsy clunk on the stone
below—you didn't hear, deflected elsewhere—
not unlike the bells I'd been hearing all along,

but clapperless, tongueless now. Anyway
you and I remain, alive, and safe.

However

I still feel the dagger's point right here at my gut,
convinced there's a mark on my skin, a purple dot,
left where the blood was raised. When I look down—
when you're not looking—, though, my eyes confirm
that there's no blade there, and no mark. But the heart
is a retina, retaining images as well as pokings
and piercings, and the mind is punctured again and again,
by the phantom of a point, the memory

of hope.

The End of Silence

Since you were silent, what other recourse
had I, blind to your cold eyes catching fire,
deaf to your voiceless ventings of—desire?
disgust? or puzzlement? I would not force
you to respond; recall, I stayed away
a good long while. But eventually,
this knowing not what you might think of me,
or us, I could not bear. Real words should say
a bit of something and thereby let out
a bit of steam. Some embers do not glow
but warmly wait for gentle breaths to blow
them back to life. Are yours like those? Without
air, ash results; without a vent, explo-
sion: Silence is not quite the same as *no!*

Cotton Candy Cancer

There are many ways to try to convey
the soughing of the wind in the cave (the cave
being the emptiness inside, a metaphor.
Now is as good a time to make that clear
as any). Here's one. You remember walking
down the boardwalk, overdosing on
cotton candy with a beloved one, talking
and laughing so easily, the sky just so,
the water bright, the sun just right,
and then, that night. . . you remember?
And then the loss? Then going back
to the same boardwalk with someone else
or alone, and ordering cotton candy
again, even though by now you are
too old for cotton candy, but for
the nostalgia, you do, and for the one you lost
who loved the stuff? And today you can't
get enough? And when you get sick,
still on the loop-de-loop, or worse, you know
you've felt like that for years? It's not
so hard to imagine. What you have is cot-
ton candy cancer, and it eats away
your insides, bit by bit by sorry bit,
and you and I have learned to live with it.

After

I visited the desert. There I saw
a skull the desert winds unsanded—or
it had a life of sorts and was trying
to re-emerge, as you've told me to do.

And everywhere the place was as a mirror;
my friends at night, moonlit, and serenaded
by the whistling wind, looked like eager corpses
walking. It was fun. It was eerie. It
was sad, for everything became a mirror
I could not keep from gazing into. When
I closed my eyes to shut it out, of course,
there was you. Then I opened them. A far-off
saguaro glowed in the dark and I blinked
and thought I saw you where it was, the height,
the dryness, and the needles. Then I blinked
again, and no, someone had placed their hat,
a hat that looked like yours, atop the wry
cactus; the breeze was slight, so didn't knock
it off, like stomach juices that churn and digest
but keep things moving downward, downward, down.

Was I in heaven, hell, purgatory,
some combination of all three, a weekend
camping trip organized to cheer me up
only succeeding in making me look
at precisely what my friends wanted to help
me not look at anymore?

But once or twice a year even the desert
is granted amnesty by heaven, which
has a good cry over something, I suppose,
and dowses the whole place with rain.
And this was that night! I lay in the open
air, opened my eyes, and noticed that all
the stars had closed their eyes as I had opened
mine, but clouds were lit by an unearthly

source, as if a city rose not far away
and its skyline illuminated upwards.
No such city was close, but the effect
was magical, as the light flicked on and off
and on again and off again, and then

I felt a drop—no, heard it
on my sleeping bag, thought it was a creature
and panicked, but with further drops,
my friends waking up and moving to the tent,
I knew, this was the night of rain. Now, rains
in deserts, I'd heard, usually start in day
because of the way the heat makes the air turn
and all that. This was a night rain—how rare!

I smiled, got soaked, and stayed in it till sunrise
when everything around—the tent, the cacti,
sand, rocks, cliffs, the very dust in the air—
glistened like a child's kaleidoscope,
or a counterpane soaked in an oily iridescence
where the oil was the Oil of Joy and Gladness I
once read about in a holy text somewhere,
and I was grateful, grateful that I had
you once—not grateful for the loss but not
so sad that it outweighed my laughter then
in the morning, in the desert, my friends asleep,
when I danced a rain dance, thoroughly improvised,
totally unnecessary. Did you send
the rain from where you are? Did you? Did you?

The Anatomy of Bliss

It's tickled me once or twice when it didn't have a head.

It's licked me now and then without a heart.

When it came in the form of an other-dimensional energy source,
    transmigrated from there to here,
It seemed to surround me in its glow
    like a warm, incandescent bath:
I wouldn't call it light because it didn't illuminate;
I wouldn't call it ectoplasm because it was alive, or seemed alive.
So alive that I felt as if another life-form
    was on the verge of hatching out of me,
    not from my rib or head or thigh but from
    all over, spontaneously generated from
joy.
Oh how it hurt with happiness.

Each time it's left me I have felt
Kinder, but ah so sadder that it had
Gone.

So it's a friendly monster, but cruel too:
    headless,
    heartless,
    bodiless,
Or all three.

Though I badly want it back
I mostly only feel its absence
Gnaw and snarl.
Mostly.

For there's remembrance
    and You
    and Now:

The out-of-body experience
That can't be
   won't be
   shouldn't be
Parsed or
Reported
Even in verse
   Like this
Which it endows with
Inscrutable

Existence.

Expectation

The first time that I saw the guy
I smiled and he winked.
I didn't know what he was try-
ing, if at all. I blinked.

The second time I saw him, he
saw me and then half-waved
and, with a finger, beckoned me.
I went and he behaved

so warmly that I felt the great
balloon inside my gut
start to fill with his warmth, inflate,
and I felt happy. But

the fifth and ninth and twelfth times that
I saw him, all he did
was nod and look away. *What?*
thought I. And then he hid.

Or sort of hid, which was much worse.
So the balloon keeps growing,
as empty as the universe,
as all the winds keep blowing.

If only he'd not thought to pick
me as one to pursue;
if only I could feel the prick
so long, long overdue,

then maybe the balloon would stop
inflating, maybe I
would celebrate to feel it pop
and be able to sigh

again. So, darling, if you find
that I don't smile or wink,

I'm cruel only to be kind.
Now dry your eyes and think:

because, you see, I sorely know
what you are going through
and would not ever want to blow
up your balloon for you.

Allegory

Why, come into the shade and rest awhile,
My dear, said the crone with the winning smile,
The sun has been burning on your face,
She purred with an other-worldly grace
In dulcimer tones, *But here, my sweet,*
You can escape from the light and heat.

So bright and so hot was the day that he,
Eyes dripping with sweat, could barely see
The thing that drew him under a tree
And into the cave of shade. They went
Deep in the dark, then she left the gent,
Stranding him there where he has spent
The oblivious life of a pampered prince,
Insignificant, ever since.

Achilles

Do not be my Patroklos! You don't need
to run off and fight foreign wars. Don't try
to enlist. I'm not invulnerable, but bleed.

And besides, just because we might not breed
genetically, well, that does not imply
you must be my Patroklos. You don't need

to lose your life with folly, prove your seed
is fertile with male arrogance. . . . Oh why
enlist? You're not invulnerable. You'll bleed—

or worse. Haven't you learned? Didn't you read
about the 'Sixties? Peace, man, Peace! Apply
the Love that made Patroklos. You don't need

this war, it isn't ours, or yours. Indeed
it hasn't been declared, though many die
to enlist, then from enlisting. Or they bleed

and come back—incomplete. Come back to bed
and let us slay that fatal notion, my
Love Soldier. And, Patroklos, should you need
to enlist, I'll be invulnerable. (But bleed.)

Cheyenne

The lightning lashed. The wind began to sting,
the sky to swirl his fingers, shades of gray.
Rational fear would have been a good thing
but they were scheduled guests on *The Today
Show* Friday, so the flight instructor let
the girl get on—and fly—the little plane.
Her parents had no fear. I can't forget
the way the windsock, rankled by the rain,

rose and fell, but they took this as a nod,
as they were going to tell America,
"She flew from California to Cape Cod!"
and everyone would gasp and ooh and ah.
Unlike Icarus, who didn't heed
his dad, she minded hers! Since she was seven,
she'll be among the cherubim in heaven,
inspiring some dark poet's ghoulish greed.

Not on the plane that day, her mom's still living,
still dreaming of her daughter there, forgiving.

Water Lilies 2

Tugged here, jerked there by quirks of a typhoon
(caprices, zeitgeists), lilies on a pond,
drawn daily, cannot help but to respond,
unmoored, moved, moving, as the feeling moon,
trapped high in the sky. Her bright appearance
adjusts as we trade studs and baubles for
new fads; she orbs and floats forevermore
professing depth of soul and free adherence
to passion, meaning—*mooning*. Then a gust
restores the matted cluster swallowing me,
of green and glimmer, whence a poet must
flex down a toe in search, invisibly—
convincing the rest of the folks that they're all free
as moonlit water lilies . . . souls . . . or dust.

Balloon

If left to its own nature, a propensity
might turn to ardor, passion, frenzy, blow
away like a child's helium balloon,
bright, free, diminishing, but visible

above. You tethered certain cravings,
but with an expandable leash, let them go
off as if by themselves, in the breeze, and high.
Then, one tug, or a few, and they were back—to hold,

exchange or re-inflate, relaunch or pop.
Advisers told you to pull down and guard
those Mylar® colors, chest them at your heart!
You turned into a six-year-old and laughed

proud of the shiny silver laced with red
bobbing in the sky for all to see.
You never saw the sense in hiding gifts.
Once, when you almost lost one in a storm,

you changed its string for cord, then sturdy rope
which dragged the air ball down—but you found this
a small price. Lately, though, recalling shrinkage
in past balloons, you've changed your mind, and at

the risk of looking like a fool, you tie
with even lighter twine and let a wind
slice each one free so it can fly away—
even from yourself—as high as the sky will allow.

Well you, my friend, my onetime reader, you
are my balloon. I lost you in a storm;
you soared beyond the rain. My only dream:
that you shall find a way back down again.

Shackles

I know where I am: I'm in the cave
where the dark is really relative,
for I study shadows that would have
us placid, and I know they give
us a sense of security that isn't real.
Well, not quite know, it's more like what I feel.
And from a distance, breezes blow
and whisper of an Elsewhere with a Would
so clearly that all my cellmates' refrains
convince me that there never were chains!
And this becomes the only thing I know:
that all my greasy dreams of rainbows could
be real—or realized—and that I should
have taken off my shackles long ago.

Lucy van Pelt

Dreaming that Schroeder loved her as his queen
she let her dreams grow into an obsession.
Then he ran off with someone seventeen
and she fell into a bout of depression
so bad her brother had to bring her to
Emergency. From there, Intensive Care.
Then they transferred her to the State Home where
she told me, when she finally realized who
I was, that she'd never even been kissed
by anyone but Snoopy. Now she lives
in the city, alone. Her therapist
tells her that only someone who forgives
herself can be healed. So she keeps a list
of faults she shows me when I am in town
and drop by. Though I wish she'd put it down,
she's almost proud of her new ones. They're all
part of the process, she says, they bring hope.

I usually bring more snapshots for her wall
of Linus, her brother, my sister Sal-
ly, and their children, who are our nephews
and nieces, but seem only to confuse
her, sometimes, they're so numerous now. *Char-
lie Brown*, she cries, through wild tears, *Charlie Brown,
you never should have let me jerk that ball.
You must hate me today!* I tell her *Nope*.

She shakes. I ease her to a seat, assure
her, *Childhood trials, they say, build character.
Don't think about it. I don't*—nor of her,
often. But I do sit with her an hour.

The Mind of the Beholder

Perhaps it is the parts that so appeal.
But every image has its implication
of deed, and piques the memory—of you
and me, or, for one inexperienced,
collective memory: of when an eye
looked back and beckoned; an arm and its hand
reached, grabbed, and held; a leg stood, turned and came;
the foot flexed, tickled, stroked, and wrapped to warm.
What is the bosom but a field of succor,
hair but a counterpane of brief abandon,
and the most private, most spectacular
of all, the very fountains of new life?

Beauty though is another thing to my
eyes—stipulating that the eyes are where
it lies—and involves doing, not just being
and letting the image imply the deed.
I've seen a bum hold a door open for
a lady passing through he'd never met,
and photographed it, and him afterwards,
all scrofulous and smiling, in a stance.
I've seen the snapshot of a matted cat
who rescued all her kittens from a blaze
one by one, risking flames and creaky beams,
and heard their still polyphony of purrs.

I recently read how Samuel picked Saul
in part for his appearance, if not all,
while David was no ugly duckling either,
and must have sung his melodies with grace
appealing to the eyes, arms, hands, legs, feet,
breast, heart, mind and fountain of everybody.
I don't think I can picture such a face,
as Michel Angelo has helped us know.
And even there, the fig leaf was applied
because the deed did not trump the image,
the whole did not exceed the parts, to some:

The salacious is in the mind of the
beholder: Puritans must be obsessed.

Appeal is most appealing when appealing
to our best, though, to our hellish, heavenly natures,
wouldn't you say? Wasn't David a hero?
And isn't that what made him beautiful?
The fact that he became a father too
might have been too much for some souls to bear,
their skin too tingly, their blood over-rushed—
unless it was that later he succumbed,
becoming an adulterer, which meant
that even heroes can think lurid thoughts.
And from his House the greatest fountains came.

But David we forgive. Can we forgive
the puritans who placed all those fig leaves,
or the prurient eyes that warranted their placement?
How else can organisms be organic,
the mind connected to the groin and deed,
part after part supportive of the whole,
the sexual a part of being human,
whole from the same root as *health* and *hole*.
And how else are we ever to become?

Lust

Your hand grips the back of your office chair
as you stand and watch the object walk
out the door, which you had kept ajar,
for propriety. You try to talk,

to summon danger back, but some
survival instinct's drained your voice.
You mouth COME BACK; O, PLEASE PLEASE COME
BACK knowing that it would not be wise.

Your palms are wet, your throat is sore.
As soon as there is no one there
your legs collapse. You close the door
then wipe your brow and the back of the chair.

You convince yourself that you are strong,
having let yet another moment pass.
Hypocrite. Coward. What's in your mind
no one else knows. How long, how long
will you be able to stay kind
and seem so calm? Tomorrow looms, alas.

House Guest

You did not look
so could not see

the drops at the edge of their smile

when you called them *good host*
spelling up whorling storms of

hypocrisy
—no, courtesy—
no, tact—

which have since left the unseen wet and strewn
within, the mess in inverse

proportion to how neat, how lush
they had made their domain, for you.

Nor did you note them since you arrived
even more obviously

still
crushed by the weight

of a perfect
pointless

halo.

Basis in Fact

You are not loved back.
It's too late to retract.
And there is no basis in fact
affecting how you feel or act
except that now the silence numbs
like nuclear attack,

or just before, your windows blacked
anticipating whatever—
but nothing comes.
The fact you're not at war, but peace,
provides you no solace,
and offers no release;

Reality's no basis
for feelings. What's more real
than what is,
is what you feel.
And it feels like it's going to feel like this
forever.

Book Sale

I got rid of all your books, and I tossed
the potted plants you tended. I was told
I had to, so I did. You never called
to say you wanted them. Now all are cast
to the winds, and thrift stores, and the compost
out back. And days, without your poems, accrue—
which is what days had been devised to do,
that we might count them, as the world grows old.

At last I figured out the vacuum and
the place is spotless now, but there was too
much room, room after room, without you,
so I bought your book. I didn't understand
a lot of it, and parts of it were sad,
but many other parts were not bad.

I Saw You

I saw you last night on the Avenue.
You didn't notice me but I saw you,
looking perfect and dapper in your walk.
You gave me, with your sureness, half a shock
as you approached. I turned to face the glass
of a store display, waiting for you to pass.
In concert with the night, you lingered there
and glanced in the same glass to adjust your hair—
it was only a wisp, a fallen lock
you tucked back. How the light became you then!
I saw your crystal cold reflection
breathe half the night in, on the verge of talk-
ing, then walk on. And once more I was free.
I'm pretty sure you didn't notice me.

Fade In/Fade Out

And now it is as if we'd never met
each other. It's as though we never knew
what we knew, quite. As though what we once were. . .
which might not have been much, but I know you

were something to me, though I'm mostly sure
what I was, you have managed to forget. . . .
But whatever it was we were, you will allow,
is nothing more than—No, it's nothing, now,

isn't it, more than a screen's dissolving image
with the chortle of a choked down memory?
I know you own no photograph of me,

nor have I looked upon your Facebook page
in years—which, I admit, *was* sweet as sin.

Since then it's been as if you'd never been.

Walt Whitman

I do not know if I did right by you.

    I held you at arm's length because
    I would embrace you, only you
were too resplendent, and people were there.

    I kept you at arm's length because
    though you had aged a birthday you
were still a protégé, and they would stare.

    I couldn't bear arm's length because
    that final day, no more were you
the protégé, and there were hours to spare.

    I wish I had you at arm's length
to ask you how your shoulders felt squeezed tight
by palms, and if you think that I did right
by you, when I was by you, should you care.

A Single Rose

I'd give a single rose but it might burn,
so put in tulips, a mixed combination,
to take space in a place they do not earn.

Add baby's breath, too, and a cooling fern,
and wrap them in dull paper, like a passion.
(I'd give a single rose, but it might burn.)

A mum? a glad? a snapdragon? Return
the tulips if you don't think it's the fashion
to take space in a place they do not earn,

and "two lips" sounds provocative. An urn
full, variegated, with a bright carnation
red as the single rose which did not burn—

a dozen different blooms, twelve ways to turn
gray in a lingering commemoration
that takes space in a place it does not earn

but is given gladly. What? I have to learn
not to care a rat's ass for reputation?
A dozen roses, then. Two. Blood red. Burn
a space in a place I know we'll never earn!

Did I react too harshly?

Did I react too harshly? What I did,
you see, is rip my heart right out—yes, reach
inside one finger at a time, squeeze each
with utmost care between adjacent ribs.
This thrilled, a little. When I flexed and grasped
an organ—well, a bloody mess—I felt
guts pumping so I knew without a doubt
it had to be a heart my hand now clasped.

I pulled and out it came. And I was fine.
I buried it nine fathoms from the sea.
The neap tide took it as a valentine,
or fish food, maybe, while the rest of me
has been adjusting, learning to survive,
not caring who suspects I'm not alive.

After I Wrote

After I wrote the poem about ripping
my heart out and burying it on a beach
where it was swept to sea, the useless thing,
I went jogging by the water one morning,
where a persistent glimmer made me reach

down. I stooped to determine what it was.
It was a heart, the size of, oh, my thumb.
A fallen earring? or a brooch? Because
the clasp was gone I wasn't sure which. Does
it matter? Silvery, tarnished, and of some

design, half of a pair or just the one:
Celtic, perhaps, its right lobe overgrown,
the left lobe, small; its inner guts a vine
of French-curved filigree swelled from within,
fresh air between the shoots. So now I own

a heart that I can leave at home or bring
along as loose as pocket change with me;
or have a jeweler set as a cheap ring
or pin; or, with a thin but strong black string,
hang over where my old heart used to be.

Tucked underneath a shirtfront, probably.

War Years

I couldn't fathom that the war years were
the *best years of his life.* That's what he'd utter,
time and again, when we'd stroll in the woods
and he'd select an unsuspecting stick,
raise it to his eye, and point
the thing: or, with his rust-nibbled pocket knife,

hack a ghost to death. He kept the knife
sharp with a strop, back and forth, as if honing were
a sacred rite, back, forth, back, testing the point,
drawing blood, sometimes. Sometimes he would utter
strange things, nothing decipherable, or jab the stick
at the air, as if meeting an enemy suddenly in the woods

overseas. He'd never come out of the woods,
I often feared. So I would steal the knife
safely back into its sheath and, unseen, stick
it somewhere he couldn't find it. These were
the frustrating memories I had of him, utter
terror, at times. But I estimated that the point

of the stick was not as dangerous as the point
of the knife. Why take him back to the woods?
I've asked myself over and over. Am I an utter
fool? But eventually his pocket knife
stayed in the sheath; we'd hike in daylight; and there were
many peaceful forest hikes. Once he took a stick

from the ground to use—as a *walking* stick,
not thinking of sharpening it. Do you see my point?
Filling his mind with good times! Though the bad times were
numerous and powerful. But by going to the woods
with him, in peace, he should forget the knife,
the war, the horrors he could never utter;

and by and by, replace the abject black with utter
light. So as for you and your friend, I say stick

to it—and to him. Hold on to objects like his knife
and gun which he might suddenly point
at *you.* Does he like walks in the woods?
Yes? Boat rides, too? You were sailors, then? Ah, you were.

Don't mind him uttering nonsense, though. The point
is that you stick with him, at sea, or in the woods.
But do take the knife: it'll remind him who you were.

Space and Fire

The feeling of the emptiness, the void,
the space, turns out to be the physical
reality of matter. Have you heard
that all that is is mostly space? All.

The distance between electrons and other
particles in an atom is as the
solar system, and galaxies. Another
pulse, another heartache, another free

spin, and you drift as a pulsar, a star,
a planet, alone, connected, disparate,
mighty, forsaken, or, if noticed, far
from the next nearest thing you can but wait

for. Quarks, electrons and the rest are on
fire, though, vivid with energy. So you,
like stars, are luminescent. Every dawn
reminds us of this, when you see night through.

And nights you'd rather not, because you feel
the synapses, the burns . . . O! Understand
I feel them too. So you can call, and we'll
stay up all night, soul to soul, hand in hand.

Beast

I've put him in a cage. He won't attack.
Come in! It's safe. I'm sure it's safe. Come in.
You want to see him? It? Him? You want to
See *me*? Come in, then. Make way. Passing through.

Come through. Come through. I don't always wear black,
No. Why'd you ask? Scotch, rye, a spot of gin?
Whatever you have I will have one too.
Good? Good. And while we're at it, how are you?

See *what* beast? Out in back? There's no "in back
Of" this house. Monster? Oh. I meant within—
Caged here, inside my—. Is it such a sin?
So sue me. But it got you here! Don't stutter.
I'd never—Sorry! Go. It's just a flutter.
I'm sure I'll manage, in a life or two.

Strange Day

I think I took the dearness
For desire,
And thought you a reflection
Not a refraction;
While you mistook my patience—deflection,
Inaction,
After that one bright night's moment of nearness—
For openness to distance,
Not that I was ever able to offer any real resistance.

No, what you clearly misconstrued
Was simply my desire not to be rude
Which acts like the opposite of desire
And is its own apostasy:
At least it was with me.

But the years' distraction
Is over. Here we are
Shattered
At a perhaps beginning, at a definite end
Somewhere between something "manqué"
And what you've called "friend."
Not that such labels will matter
Or ever should have mattered—
Nor that I know whether it's more the former or the latter.

It is a strange day
At the onset of such a change.
Gratefully, I don't mind
Only, strangely, find
You strange
As a curio on a shelf
And myself
As one with nothing more to say.

These Tears

Some tears are formed from what hearts feel,
while others well from what eyes see
or from tricks of the mind. Mine reveal
    a little of all three.

Some fall as water droplets, clear
and brief as a seducer's wink.
Others may last: You have one here
    that's turned from blood to ink,

the recreation of drops shed
rendered anew in red and black.
Page seven's where I wished you dead;
    one hundred, wished you back.

What's to forgive, what's to forget,
that I should not immortalize?
For these tears, since we've never met,
    fell from my pen, not my eyes.

Mean Drunk

I used to remember the grand times we had,
Reminiscences happily saved.
But of late I look back on the deeds you did,
For an honester path has been paved.

O it's burned me to walk it, Father-o'-mine
From my crinkling toes to my head,
And admit that my world has turned almost fine
Now that you are dead.

Our marshland romps, our woodland drives,
Our treks to St. Augustine,
O the Christmas rites—and "Indian Guides"?—
You were our leader, then.

But you also kicked Mother down the stair—
And for nothing she had said
Or done—You don't remember? Sure
You don't, now that you're dead.

You did it once when I was three,
Twice when I was five,
Et cetera. In front of me. She
Managed to survive.

Then, back when you abandoned us
And left my brothers and me
To mercurial adolescences
Of sordid secrecy

I thought it was the worst of acts
That any dad could do.
I see now, reassessing facts,
That wasn't so, with you.

For as we began to live our lives
Without vermouth and gin,

We lost, at last, our fear of knives,
And of tempers you'd be in.

I sort of suspected you wouldn't recall
Those hells you brought to light,
So I kept them in a diary—all,
That is, since I could write.

Now I've compiled them in list form,
In large font and bright ink
For you to read. They'll keep you warm
For centuries, I should think.

                        Envoi

If you are a father, dear reader, I write
These lines for you as a warning.
If you've ever "blacked out" what you did some night
When you tried to arise the next morning,

Someone, no doubt, was there with you
And saw you at your most rotten,
To whom you'll account for the deeds you do,
Even those you've "forgotten."

And if it's a son with a taletelling heart
And a mind overgiven to thinking,
He is doomed—unless you do your part
And curb   your   drinking.

                                      after Sylvia Plath

Old Folks' Home

Their slowing down can be like needles in
the eyes, or in your heart, if a loved one.
Why go there, then, to visit strangers who
all say they're *just fine*, whenever I ask?
For schadenfreude? No! For inspiration!
Their inner gears clank with, let's call it, rust
that's irremovable. Mine, only frost.
So in the absence of a summer sun,
slowed by the aftermath of one love lost,
I find it a convenient place to bask,
that frozen gears, like memories of you,
might melt—or I, as easily, adjust.

I didn't mind

I didn't mind it when you called me Dirt,
for dirt is soil (my bed is rich and soft)
and tears are seeds. (Come, show me where you hurt.)

The first time, we were teen-aged. Green. I flirt-
ed back. You didn't notice. I was daft
and didn't mind much if you thought me dirt

(which in a way I was). How you avert-
ed every glance, then. But, though Art and Craft
turn tears to seeds, the planting ought to hurt,

some, no? ("No pain, no gain.") So every curt
retort of yours, I noted as I laughed,
but didn't mind, much, learning to sling dirt

back, while you learned to take it like a sport.
Till now. The "Great Love of your Life" has left.
What tears! (What seeds!) But you would never hurt

this much, you crowed, once, didn't you, My Heart?
Yes—that is how I've thought of you. How oft-
en? Always, since that day you called me Dirt.
Such tears are seeds. Come. Show me where you hurt.

Stupid Questions

There are no stupid questions,
only stupid people
who say stupid things
like "That's a stupid question,"
and make a loved one miserable
as I just did.

Cutting Board

    Too much thought about what never happened
    makes it better that it never happened.

What do you do when that Someone whistles
into your everywhere and, like
a gust of wind, makes you gasp
from your very core, your lungs, your cave?
Then they speak, and a saw-toothed pennant
    flaps around in your
        everywhere.

    A simple knife would be cleaner, clearer, easier.

Their wit's like a click from amber to green,
you're sure, the signals clear enough
that you know to hold in the cyclone heroically,
out of courtesy, for a while
    until

    that Someone turns in a flash to Someone Else.

In time the wind-flag stops and droops
ossified into a board—
it feels almost as if the thing
were never there at all, as if
that Someone never were, only
this Someone Else, cold, dry, still. . . .

    Too much thought about what never happened
    makes it wiser that it never happened.

Then Someone suddenly reappears
by cursed coincidence and tells
you after all these years they *need you*.
You've nothing at home, nothing inside,
    but invite them over—O, to entertain.

So much thought about what never happened
makes it happier that it might happen.

The wind in the cave bats the board
around and it pierces ten times as bad
as it did when it was but cloth. The less
you want the more it seems you need,
as you lay crudités with a calculated
order to their rawness: fresh
pepper, red to the eye but cool
to the tongue; cucumber, complacent in
    its skin, angled to slice
        what a metaphor. . . .

You serve not knowing the knife's still
in your hand, too close to your guest's left ear.
Noticing it, you're sure you won't
be entertaining like this again
    lest

    Too much thought about what must not happen
    makes it far too likely that it happen.

Band-Aids®

Why did the Johnsons or the Curads ever
think to make their strips the color
of skin (well, Caucasian skin)?
I'd think a wound would better heal
if sealed in a bright, garish, opposite hue,
purple, green, heliotrope, or blue
so passersby might see that you'd been wounded, and where,
and refrain from grabbing and squeezing or slapping or
scratching you there.

And as goes the flesh, so goes the spirit,
so goes the heart: If only we *could*
affix a flagrant and gaudy bandage
where we've bled and grown scabs, not so that
one might bring up the dark topic of how
the wound happened, but so that, without a word,
we might re-immerse in a world of people,
friends and strangers, and not worry so much
about being unintentionally slapped or scratched
in the unreal felt place deep within,
right where— . . . Well, haven't you lived this yourself?
Haven't you had to leave a room, suddenly,
when no one had the least idea of why?

Some gashes like that, hueless and invisible,
seem to bleed and bleed, never stopping,
and get deeper and deeper and deeper and deeper
and deeper and deeper and deeper.

Torn

If, in a *billet-doux*, you made a blunder
but caught the gaffe in time, you could reject
it, once upon a time, sliding it under
your blotter to revise, throwing it away,
or tearing it to smithereens outright
so that no passing soul should ever suspect
the passing feeling, penned, oblitera-
ted, as paper tears and burns. On Valentine's Day
my basket used to overbrim in white
and red. On one occasion, I repaired
the sin and sent it; I loved the creativ-
ity, and shocking myself that I dared
to dabble with that other way of liv-
ing—offering all, full speed ahead,
in drastic cursive ink on white and red.

Now, when I save an email as a Draft,
it's far less dire than tearing cards to pieces,
and less exhilarating, but only a dope
would share some of the red-tinged tropes I write
(like what I scribbled and destroyed tonight)
without suspecting I was, at the very least, daft.
But as My Drafts o'erteems, and as release is
essential to recovery, every now
and then I will delete the file. Or not:

For if a finger lingers, and I happen to op-
en and look, before deleting, at what I'd forgot-
ten, nearly, and feel a rush of ridiculous hope,
which the human in me can't help but allow,
the drought's quenched, and the blood's aboil again,
tearing a soul in two to crave a pen
and paper, red and white, that we might think,
not merely feel. So keep this testament
of you and me not as a file unsent,
but, since a solid document, in ink,

semi-immortal, if more stained than pure,
as an Act of God, or Love, or Literature.

Spite 2

The battery that keeps one running even
when unplugged for so long
absent an other-worldly event
to bestow one with the fortitude of God.
Not the opposite of grace, therefore, but plainly
its surrogate.

Since you've come into the picture, however,
it's what makes one act regardless of tremors.
Not the opposite of love, therefore, but plainly
its interlocutor.

Wherever you twirl, I know there is no
pot of gold, nor fleece, only
anticipation
of falling off
a precipice. But there
I go, to the top
of the cliff, to the middle
of you, in spite
of the height, in spite
of the whirlpool, in spite
of myself, in spite
of all.

Again

Again
I am not
Like so many yesterdays
When you've gone
By
One turned and looked and
I saw the one and
Again

I was not
Like so many tomorrows that were
The yesterdays to come
And now
Beneath the wasnot
And the shallnotbe
I am not
Again
As one turns and looks and
I see the one and
You are going
By
And I

Am only a half a tenth
An nth
Of Us and We
For me
And Our and My
Is Ours
For hours
O
Until you go

Again
And I
Am
Not

Yet Another Day

You thought about not setting the alarm or
of drowning in a snifter or a phial
last night but laid your suit and tie like armor
again, numbly, acceding for the while,
      existing.

The morning rings. You stir and try
not to imagine saws like *Put
your best foot* . . . Well. A voice nags, *Why?*
Why not, you snap back, forwarding your foot,
      resisting.

Left. Right. Right, left. What mattered once, does not.
You're rusted with experience and too clever,
till a whisper says, *Be glad of what you've got.*
You've got to scream—yet glory in the noise
you make, smile for no reason whatsoever,
and laugh like an infant crawling in his toys,
      persisting.

Race

He spent his life developing this car:
His green years dedicated to design;
Then crafting it in silver like a star
With one red stripe, red like a valentine
For—Well, you've just told me you never knew,
But now it is too late for honesty,
Since here he lies commemorating—you.
Reflected in the metal I can see,
No longer glowing in an innocence,
But next to his, some slivers of your face
Painted in red and silver shards with dents.
I'll take one as a token of this race.
You take one, too, a mark of excellence.
And let us place them in some cherished place.

A Difficult Parting

Life leaves, in fine,
but does not then betray
like a bittersweet love
still fond, but not to have.

It just leaves
no tears, no blame
just as death is
death.

Do not accuse me
then of treachery,
you who convinced me once
I was your life,

but let me go
for tears will irrigate
as blame will raise a spark
and reignite.

veil

Lift it gently up,
the veil of appearances—
Risk the agony:

Seeing unfiltered.
Lift it gently up again—
Risk the ecstasy:

Feeling every breeze
on your moistened face—Being:
stung by sweet storms

Weight

If we were in The Cave enchained
    the chains were of our making,
the iron ball, no ball at all,
    the heaviness, imagined.
I too had grown complacent there
    until I went spelunking
and through a crack of darkness, spied
    a glimmer winking through:
I leapt to see if I could reach
    it, fell. This weight was real,
the weight of me, my body, brought
    to light by the desire
to reach the higher, brighter place
    just within my sight;
to freely bask, and breathe, and walk,
    and ease the heft, with light.

Fiasco

They'd said goodbye forever the night before,
babbling like fools in—
                      Keep this a simile;
he had affection, but not a lover's: more
like gelatin just poured but still unset,
the flavored liquid stirred and steaming yet.

He attributed the chance to some sort of
a synchronicity, cosmos-inspired,
next day, as if the gods mocked, or were tired
of their morbidity. For love is love:

Who was to say but them what was to be?
And it worked. They laughed, and with a hug or two,
said good bye again, warmly and happily,
with a "Till next time" and a "Later, you."

Then on his lingering, final "Gotta go,"
the other chimed in with "Parting is such. . . ."
forgetting those were words to Romeo
from Juliet. Well he made overmuch

of this, the wretch. The sweetness and that sorrow
were nothing of course to the present fiasco:
The quote was from a lover, was it not,
giving him leave to feel? Well, so he thought

and dove right down and loved not like but as
a fool "too fond" (that's Juliet's) as he was
too honest; but only because—
                          only because
he mistook the meaning in a chance event
and misconstrued a citing's cool intent

not loving first, but, loved, over-requiting,
unable to stop, even when it proved

hopeless. To know him then, you'd have been moved and recommended that he take up writing.

Book Jackets

A love that's kept unheard of
may dry the lust, in time,
but meanwhile send a word of
its provenance, in rhyme

for someone else to mention
and laugh, or read aloud
that others pay attention,
some smattering of proud

self-described poetry lovers
who'll never buy the book,
but flip through bargain covers
and think they've had a look.

Still, thank you for the listen;
it's made this missive beam,
these raiments, tickled, glisten,
and cleaner than a dream.

The Quickest Way

The quickest way from
Me to You, Imagination,
is Our enemy.

Dance et Cetera

When I dance my soul dances too.
I cannot dance in fact without my
    soul and mind dancing too.
If you dance with me you dance with my
    soul and mind and heart, too.
Won't you dance with me (and my
    soul and mind and heart and breath,
        etc.)?

When I dance my arms dance too.
I cannot dance in fact without my
    arms and legs dancing too.
If you dance with me you dance with my
    arms and legs and fingernails and toenails, too.
Won't you dance with me (and my
    arms and legs and fingernails and toenails
        and corns and bunions and warts and moles
            and cellulite,
                etc.)?

Defiance

When the one you love doesn't love you back
Will the sun go dim and the world turn black
Or can you turn the love you think
You suffer from, with a magic BLINK,
To like? This phase is, after all,
But the beginning of the fall—
A fall I know only too well
When I think of how frequently I fell
When I lived here. But I moved away
To a plusher place and survived that day.
Now I'm about to take a hike
In the hills with the one I used to like—
But I live by going and going back
And defying the world to turn jet black.

                                                after Dorothy Parker

Hel—

once a darkling goddess, fed
by all those who've left me
despairing, driven, live but dead,
like a divinity—

has since become a nightly inn
where cresseted desire
makes stunning streaks on inmates' skin
set aglow by fire.

But just as poets feed the flame
to stoke an embered soul
so chefs and bakers need the same
to create at all.

Photographers meanwhile amaze
with side-effects of night:
beauty's the effect of blaze,
torch or candlelight

upon a moistened, mourning cheek;
the tear escapes detection,
its course too brief, its voice too weak,
but what divine reflection!

That's why a living hell like this,
my dear, I cannot rue,
any more than the first kiss
I received from you.

Dreams should fly

Dreams should fly.
That's what they do.
That's half the purpose of the sky.

Eventually,
though, you must land,
for if you fly incessantly

when you're born
with legs and arms
you will grow tired and worn:

Unbearable
almost
as no dreams at all.

Look at me
and learn, for that's
half the point of poetry:

Dreams and hope
bring hurricanes
unless you come to pause and cope.

O walk a bit,
sit, rest.
We might even talk a bit.

And the air,
after all,
isn't going anywhere.

Retort to an Outgoing Love

I'll jump in the lake, as you've requested—
Anything to satisfy.

Has the water, though, been tested?
If the water be infested
You, my Dear, would be arrested
Should I deign to soothe your ache,
Do what you say, jump in the lake
And die.

Give me another command, though,
And I'm your servant
Foolish and fervent
In love and sin
As I've always been,
My Dear, my Hell,

As you know
Only too well.

At Last

I met him at last
Oasis to my desert
White knight and black knight in one

Alpha and omega
Night and day
My everything, a walking poem

Dangerous, but
A harbor. A gentleman
Wild as the unknown seas.

Had you met him, you'd
Have told me he's perfect
What I'd needed all along

Even as
I'd given up
Looking, caring or hoping.

He opened the side
Of me I was
Sure was closed and dead

With him, I lived
For the first time, it seemed,
Knew why I was slapped on earth

And started to write
Ridiculous poetry
And understood jumping off roofs.

Once he brought me
Back to life
I started, however, wondering

About horizons
And possibilities
And what the rest of our lives together

Might mean. Which got
Me to looking around
At other knights on steeds

And the whole blooming
World looks
Good

And the everything knight
Who started it all
Has become a lot like me

As I used to be,
That is, save
That he doesn't write poetry

And must be watched
On moonlit nights
When he climbs up to the roof.

Furnace

The inner vault of experience, which I have stoked
with what I have produced, or felt, or lived—
I won't say there is a treasure trove in there;
as a matter of fact, I can't say what there is.

It feels as if it's been expanding every
day and I am larger than I've ever
been, inside, but don't know if I'm stuffed
with oxygen, ether, or absence—emptiness—

till you walk by and turn and look and touch
a face, like this. My face. Or wink. Or issue
some other such spark that drops in and either dowses
or ignites the dry tank instantly to flames
if not a whole new universe.

If it glimmers, if it shines, there's a furnace at its heart.

Fireflies

My loves have been like fireflies—bright and cold,
when what is wanted is a warmth. Like stars,
which everybody loves—but who can hold
one? No one has. So I have shelves of jars,

glass jars, mementos of the times I've leapt
to seize a star but gotten a firefly
instead (as opposed to the nights I've slept
instead of being drawn by the night sky

outdoors). What do you feed a firefly, though?
I've asked around but no one knows. Do you?
I didn't think so. So this jar will go
dark as the rest in, oh, a day or two.

And each one has a label with its date
of capture, and a name to correspond
to someone loved, whom I commemorate,
or someone of whom I was at least fond.

I never use ball point, but India ink
to fill the label out, against the white;
this makes each name indelible, I think.
Yours is still drying, which is only right.

After Rain

      Even a leafless tree
Will shimmer in a desolate dew
      Even a forest charred
      Will glisten after a rain

      After a realm is razed
One day a cricket chirps again
      One night a lightning bug
      Succeeds in shining through.

      Since lands after a blaze
Might not sustain a single soul
      And skies might stay a haze
      Of embers caked as coal

      Maybe we need the rain
To wash us off and wash away
      The sereness and the stain
      Day after dark after day.

      But after the rain, to-night,
I saw a single firefly's light:
      It drenched me, not with warmth,
      But O such life.

My Heart has Been

My heart has been an orchard—
Plush. pruned. picked. unpicked—
Through which I too can stroll through files
Of fulsome fallen fruit

Today I stoop to reach for one
Half-buried in the dirt
Where from the rich cool darkling dirt
It's sprouted a first leaf

Just as the name of one I loved
Glistens on the spine
Of a volume sweet and tart as souls
Waiting to be known

Terrains congeal in winter
As the bereft endure
Grand passions of the seasons
Let loose upon the world

So fruit trees will emancipate
Their unculled purposes
And long lost loves will germinate
Orchards of their own

Fast and Furious

When we met and fell
I said, "Never before . . . "
Our love was so great,
And new.

When it ended like hell
I swore, "Nevermore
Shall I love like that."
. . . You?

                                                  after Robert Graves

Weston

I turned left onto Love,
which runs half-parallel to Pine,
with Highland the connecting link,
on a morning walk of mine,

and thought of those whom I have loved
and those for whom I'd pined.
Then I thought, "I've walked the High Land,"
and I felt that I felt fine

because the light was low and cool
and sweetened so the day:
and every road, including Love,
had taken me this way.

Note:

To borrow a phrase from film credits, please be aware that no actual person, living or dead, should be construed as represented in these poems. The verse has been hewn out of welters of experience fertilized by imagination—and vice versa.

Thank you for visiting.

—JBN

Another note:

For multi-page poems in this collection, stanzas continue from the bottom of one page to the top of the next—except for pages 5-7, 43-44, 77-78 and 98-99, where each page starts a new stanza, but the blank lines normally indicating this have been eliminated by the pagination.

James B. Nicola's poetry books are more than collections; each one takes the reader on a particular journey with a beginning, middle and end. *Manhattan Plaza* (2014) thus "reads like a biography or memoir . . . with the thoughtfulness of an architect's blueprint or a tour guide's Baedeker," according to *Vermont Literary Review,* while *Great Weather for Media* observes that *Stage to Page: Poems from the Theater* (2016) "illustrates a life in the theatre, warts and all" and "would recommend [it] not only to readers . . . but also to poets who are interested in developing collections which follow a specific theme."

His individual poems have appeared stateside in the *Antioch, Southwest* and *Atlanta Reviews, Rattle, Tar River,* and *Poetry East*, and in many journals in Europe and Canada. A Yale graduate, he won a Dana Literary Award, a *Willow Review* award, and a People's Choice award (from *Storyteller*), and he was featured poet at *New Formalist*. His nonfiction book, *Playing the Audience,* won a *Choice* award.

Following the tradition of poets Stanley Kunitz, Elizabeth Bishop, and Frank O'Hara, James moved from his native Worcester, Massachusetts, to New York City where he makes his home. Lately he has been conducting both theater and poetry workshops at libraries, literary festivals, schools, and community centers all over the country, most notably the Kennedy Center/American College Theater Festival.

James is also a director, composer, lyricist, and playwright. His children's musical *Chimes: A Christmas Vaudeville* premiered in Fairbanks, Alaska, where Santa Claus was rumored to be in the audience on opening night.

www.ingramcontent.com/pod-product-compliance
Lightning Source LLC
Chambersburg PA
CBHW070548090426
42735CB00013B/3114